Six Simple Steps to Success

Directed by Purpose

How to Focus on Work That Matters, Ignore Distractions and Manage Your Attention over the Long Haul

Written and Published By: Michal Stawicki

"Efforts and courage are not enough without purpose and direction."
– John F. Kennedy

Table of Content

It's a Zombie World!

As I write these words, I'm on a crowded train, commuting from work to home. In the compartment, there are about 100 people. Half of them are playing with their mobiles. Some of them are napping. Some are staring blankly outside. Several are chatting with the strangers they've found themselves sitting beside today.

The man next to me might well be immersed in deep prayer or contemplation. But I wouldn't bet money on that. He is looking out the window, trailing his eyes across the view without registering anything.

I have a déjà vu moment.

About a year ago, I was traveling on a different train in a smaller compartment. There were just eight of us. It was five or six in the morning. We were commuting to the capital to start our day at work. My co-passengers were all asleep. I was doing the work I love—writing another book. It was work, nonetheless.

Look around you. How many people are in this exact moment fulfilling their life purpose? How many of them are 100% focused on the job at hand because they believe the task is a necessary part of their life's journey? How many are pursuing—at this very moment—their vision for life?

(If you are alone, do this exercise by recalling a moment when you were last in a group.)

It's likely that few are pursuing any kind of purpose or vision. You may be idealistic and give many of these people the benefit of the doubt, but if you had to stake all your savings on the answer, what percentage would you assume?

As I write these words, I am pursuing my vision in this train compartment right now. I doubt there are more than three other people who could say the same about themselves.

Face it: we live in a zombie world. Zombie Apocalypse has already happened. Millions—or billions—of people wander around without any deeper sense of mission than to get through the current day. They stare emptily into televisions and tablets or tap gossipy texts into their mobiles. They anesthetize themselves with alcohol, drugs, video games, and other physical or mental substances to avoid thinking at all.

Mindless consumption is the new overpowering imperative.

These zombies also suck at the brains of those who still live fully, trying to involve them in the same mindless activities. They can't stand anyone who claims there is higher purpose and meaning to human life.

Did you found those words a little strong? Don't think I'm pointing fingers. I was a zombie myself until quite recently. I know how it feels. It stinks.

I began to awaken in August 2012. Life has been continuously invigorating since then.

Zombie Jobs

Surveys and statistics tell us this: only 30% of people in the United States are satisfied with their jobs. Think about that. Seven out of ten people only do the work they do because of the paycheck they receive. Doesn't that waste of potential break your heart?

But wait a moment. Those figures are from the USA; they are higher than anywhere else. In the rest of the world, even fewer people are satisfied with what they do in their earning hours. Taking into account the time necessary for sleep and other basic routines, dissatisfied people are spending more than two thirds of their lives being miserable.

Why does our society think this is all right? Every individual has a different story, but this extraordinary statistic is the result of a culture—our culture—that values things, not ideas. If you have the newest model of sports car, many sins will be forgiven in the eyes of a consumer-focused society. Having a noble character doesn't hurt your likability… but to be considered successful, you'll also need a shiny house, a yacht, and a Mercedes.

Wise (and happy) people discovered thousands of years ago that the source of success and happiness is within ourselves.

"Happiness depends upon ourselves." – Aristotle

"True happiness is... to enjoy the present, without anxious dependence upon the future." – Lucius Annaeus Seneca

"There is only one way to happiness and that is to cease worrying about things which are beyond the power of our will." – Epictetus

"Blessed is anyone whose conscience brings no reproach and who has never given up hope." – Sirach 14: 2

A few in each generation discover this anew. But most are miserable, or merely unhappy, because they look for fulfillment in things. They constantly seek new external stimulation; they chase new shiny objects.

Unfortunately, if you have ever overdone any stimulant in the past—had too much to drink or overeaten—you'll know that an excess of external stimuli doesn't bring more than momentary happiness.

To find fulfillment, we must find our own reasons for being, and then act accordingly. I'm not saying that you have to become a monk in a contemplative order, although that's definitely an alternative worth considering. It isn't for me; I decided to get married many years ago and that path is now closed. Your current choices are affected by your past choices.

There are a few rare occupations in which you can unite every possible human aspiration: **spiritual enrichment, great health, deep relationships, constant progress, recognition from others,** and **wealth**. But usually you can get only a piece of that perfect pie and will yearn for the rest. And even if you are seeking only money from your job, most roles are not a path to wealth.

Examine your job. Which of those elements do you find in it? Not even one? Or are there a few? Then ponder the next question: what's more important, your job or those missing elements? Job or health? Job or relationships? Job or your soul?

You probably see where I'm heading. No wonder most of us are miserable! We spend half of our lives (or more) doing things that don't fulfill us. How the heck can you be happy and successful when you have no time to do things that *will* bring success and happiness?

It is not our jobs *per se* that make us miserable. There are also a lot of entrepreneurs who feel enslaved to their businesses. And a sizeable 30% *are* satisfied with their jobs.

Purpose and Success

Consider this simple principle: either you are focused on your goals and dreams and spend your time pursuing them, or you are not. Success won't materialize out of the blue one day and land on your doorstep. You must work to achieve it.

What about the ones who have found a way to focus on what matters? They are the ones we might call successful. They work with passion. When they do their jobs, whether for themselves or for others, they aren't just "going through the motions" to get money at the end of the month. They have fulfilling occupations that encompass more than just the "wealth" part of their life.

Entrepreneur Pat Flynn works from a home office; he finds it a simple way to marry work and family. He can spend much of his day with his kids. Plus, he just loves what he is doing, which is helping other people to become online entrepreneurs. My friend Matt Gibbs, who transformed his health, now has a personal training business because he wants to share with the whole world his newly discovered excitement about being healthy.

These two men do the things they love. They would happily do them for free. Both did, for some time. Pat created his first website to help himself and others pass a difficult architecture exam. Matt organized Nordic walking lessons just to share his passion.

One of the alternative definitions of success I've encountered is: *"Success is doing what you love, even if nobody pays you for what you are doing."* But there's a paradox I find amusing. It's difficult to do something from your whole heart and not be rewarded in financial terms. Pat earns over $100,000 a month. Matt has his own successful business.

I've been able to observe—from a close perspective—other such stories. Another friend, Mark Messick, is an author. Pick any of his books and read just a few pages; you'll notice he is a passionate fellow. His income from royalties is very impressive for a teenager.

Starla Rich is a woman I admire. She suffers from many health issues. That hasn't broken her spirit. She started "Encouraging Enterprises," a movement to inspire other people to dream and follow those dreams. She started a blog and a Facebook community, charging nothing for her comments and advice. Down the road, an opportunity opened. She was invited to write articles about health in a big magazine. Now she is a contributor and earns money from her articles.

In 2012, I was 33 years old. I had no idea what I was doing on this planet. I lived day by day just to get by. And then I read the book that changed my thinking and my life. About two months after finishing that book, I realized I wanted to write.

It took me another couple of months to start my first blog. In less than ten months, I'd earned my first buck from writing. Twenty months on, I earned in one month an amount equal to half my monthly salary from my day job.

Fast-forward one more year ... and in one month I earned *more* than the salary from my day job.

When you have a vision for your life and work towards it purposefully with a diligent focus, it's very hard not to get compensated. And more than that, when you connect to your deepest desires and do something every day to realize them—while enjoying the process—you are already happy and successful.

It's the world that successful people know. They wake up each day with positive anticipation.

The basic difference between zombies and successful people is the source of their inspiration and motivation. Successful people find inspiration in their souls. They are obsessed by what they can do for other people and this kind of motivation comes solely from within.

But the most striking difference between those who are miserable and those who are happy is that happy people display vision. Successful people know where they are heading. They don't sit on their hands and wait for a sudden surge of inspiration. They feed their inspiration with constant action. Their vision drives them to do the necessary tasks.

If you work consistently, you are bound to get results. It is as simple as that. And having a vision you passionately desire helps maintain constancy. You won't chase one thing today and another tomorrow. You'll steadily march in one single direction. It's difficult to miss your destination when you act in such a manner.

Vision fuels focus, which generates action. Action brings results.

That's the "secret" behind success.

Chapter TWO

Understanding Focus

Why is focus important?

Because focus determines what gets done. Yes, everyone is doing things, and many are very, very busy. But despite this, almost all are unhappy on some level because they spend too much of life chasing dreams that are not their own. They are focused on the wrong things.

Most of us want to satisfy our spouse or parents. We want to look good in the eyes of others. We spend time building the careers and fortunes of our bosses at work ... And 95% of us get just enough to sustain our minds and bodies for the next day's existence.

Billionaires and millionaires are focused on their own purposes, on their own mission.

All successful people are laser-focused; many try to teach their students to put focus first and foremost. John Lee Dumas, who started a daily podcast from scratch and developed his business to seven figures within a couple of years, promotes the concept that focus is a source of success.

One of the first rules that race car drivers are taught is to look in the direction that you want the car to go. When traction is lost, all the learned techniques come into play, and muscle memory can make them automatic. Only if they are focused on the exact destination they need to go will all those techniques avoid a crash and get them back on the right course.

But even with compelling role models like John, I'm not convinced to turn away from many of my daily activities, simply to focus on one. A human being comprises body, mind, and spirit, and I'm interested in developing myself in each of these areas.

I dedicate about one hour a day to my spiritual life by reading, praying, meditating, and a few other activities. As far as my health goes, I continually challenge myself and have beaten about 100 personal fitness records, lost over 10% of my body weight, and drastically changed my diet and eating patterns.

They are ALL important to me. I am not willing to quit on my family, my church community, my business, or my exaggerated personal development program. I feel like a part of me would die if I did.

My theory is that time multiplied by attention equals results.

TIME * ATTENTION = RESULTS

Both factors (time and attention) are finite. The more you give of your time or your attention to a specific project, the faster your results will materialize. If you disperse your efforts over a long period of time or you dedicate just short bursts of activity to any project, you'll get fewer or smaller results.

The same goes with your attention: if you spread it too thinly over several activities, you'll still get results in each area, but each will be smaller than if you focused your attention on just one thing.

According to my equation, I receive results in each area I dedicate time and attention towards. These results will be individually smaller than if I focused in one area. As long as I fuel the left part of my equation with a constant contribution of my time and attention, the right part will take care of itself.

The biggest danger of dispersion is discouragement. It happens to many of us. We get excited about an idea, try it for some time, don't get results, or judge the effects inadequate, and quit. We don't give up on our dreams, however. We switch to another "better" method that looks promising. We live in a constant "switch state," never putting in enough time and attention to any given way of achieving our goal.

I don't get discouraged. I stick with my daily disciplines day in and day out for months and years. That's why I have been able to observe results in many realms, like spirit or fitness. But I'm insanely stubborn.

For the majority, who are not stubborn, motivation to continue is dependent on results. Focusing on one area gives the maximum possible results in that field. That is why a focus on the single most-important area is often the best solution.

Filters in Your Brain

You need focus, because your brain is a gigantic filtering mechanism. Your brain registers everything happening around you. Every smell, move, color, noise, change in temperature. The power of the wind and the level of natural or artificial light. Every single thing.

Your mind receives over 100 million sensory inputs every second. In order to keep your feeble mind sane, the vast majority of these impulses are filtered out. To achieve your mission or purpose, you need to put this enormous filtering capability to use.

Like a small steering wheel directs the rudder of gigantic transatlantic ships, your focus directs your subconscious mind. From these 100 million impulses, it begins to pick those that are in accordance with your attention. You start receiving the data you need from the vast ocean of information your senses register.

Goals are one of the tools you can use to achieve focus. Another is passion. Using them in combination work best. Frankly, I can't imagine achieving goals in the long run without at least a pinch of passion for them.

For example, I have a goal of growing my email list. From a technical point of view, it's a tiring task. Setting up the list involves forms, landing pages, testing— it's all time-consuming and arouses no passion at all in me. And while I know an email list serves a higher purpose by helping build my business, building business for the sake of it doesn't motivate me much.

My real passion when it comes to growing my email list is meeting new people. I love to connect with my readers. Their stories and gratitude are so rewarding. This is really what keeps me glued to those technical activities.

If you are interested in the "Time" part of the equation, in sticking with your habits long enough to observe the results, I elaborated on that in *The Art of Persistence.*

This book provides you the tools for the "Attention" part of the equation. The things I discuss—vision, purpose, mission and your personal mission statement, goals, motivation, and more—will help you install permanent filters in your brain. Those filters will work in the background to help you focus by shifting your attention to what's really important, not just urgent or shiny.

If you have no preferred method of focusing yourself, try them one by one and see what works for you. For a method to be successful, it must provide results (increased focus) and you must be comfortable with it.

How comfortable? Well, the prospect of practicing this particular method every day for the next ten years shouldn't send a cold shiver down your spine. In fact, ten years is the least imaginable period for me. This focus tool should serve you for the rest of your life.

Part I
What is the Value of Purpose?

(Chapter THREE)

Definition of Purpose

Let's look at the meaning of this word. The word **purpose** comes from the Anglo-French *purpos* "intention, aim, goal," and from the Old French *porpos* "aim, intention."

The origin (etymology), and my intuition, tells me that purpose is something all encompassing and overarching. Purpose is "big picture."

Let's dive deeper into the definition of purpose:

1. The reason for which something is done or created or for which something exists.

2. A person's sense of resolve or determination.

Your purpose gives you a drive to act. Purpose stirs emotions that get you up and get you going. Without purpose, your motivation to act is weak, and you will only move if an external force pulls or pushes you. As soon as this force ceases, your action will cease too. But if you have purpose, you continue on, no matter what is going on around you.

This isn't just theoretical. There were (and still are among us) plenty of people whose achievements seem to be beyond the stretch of normal human ability.

Let's look at some big figures of the 20th century: Nelson Mandela, Ronald Reagan, Mahatma Gandhi, Martin Luther King. Their deeds seem well beyond the norm, as if taken straight from a Hollywood blockbuster. But when you take a closer look, you will notice each had a burning desire, a purpose.

21

I write on Quora.com. When I began contributing to that site, I saw that people were hungry for motivation. Inspired by stories about the world's leaders, they attempt to act in a similar fashion. But purpose is not something you chase, it is something you discover. Imitating brings faux-purpose, which isn't fulfilling. When people try to use secondhand purpose, they get discouraged and cease to believe there is any meaning to life.

I'm a student of saints. They fascinate me. I've read dozens of texts written by saints. I can see how purpose radiated in their lives. It was their ultimate motivation for the incredible sacrifices they made. Many of them served in very difficult circumstances for an extended period of time. Service wasn't a one-time occurrence, it was their everyday bread.

I'm encouraged by the achievements of saints because they were ordinary people. Certainly, some, like Saint John Paul II, were very gifted individuals. Saint John Paul II knew several languages and his IQ may have qualified him for Mensa. But many saints grew up with little education; they had no advantages. They had only a strong sense of purpose.

Blessed Mother Teresa from Calcutta was a simple nun; she believed her purpose was to help the poor in India and, later, in the whole world. Saint Faustina Kowalska came from a poor peasant family; her purpose was demonstrating the power of God's mercy to the world. If you ever have a chance to read her diary, you'll immediately notice what a simple soul she was.

Those are just two examples among many others. There is nothing special about a saint, but they and the leaders I mentioned earlier had world impact because their drive to serve was deeper than any superficial motivation. It came from purpose.

(Chapter FOUR)

There are Three Ways to Find Purpose

Victor Frankl, a brilliant 20th century psychologist, defined three states of existence through which people can distill the meaning of their lives.

1. Love

If you truly love, you may need little else for fulfillment. Many of the people revered as saints found purpose through showing love.

But secular people change lives with love too. Martin Luther King, Mahatma Gandhi, and Nelson Mandela were all people driven by their deep reservoirs of compassion. They achieved a lot in their lives—two of them became heads of state—but their main motivation for acting day to day wasn't the achievement of power or success but the love for their people.

Many ordinary people share this trait. Victor Frankl believed he was saved from near-certain death in a concentration camp by his love for his wife. I know a few people—I'm sure you do too—whose strong love for their immediate family is apparent to anybody who meets them.

To properly express your love, you need to take a ton of action. As the apostle put it:

"If one of the brothers or one of the sisters is in need of clothes and has not enough food to live on, and one of you says to them, 'I wish you well; keep yourself warm and eat plenty,' without giving them these bare necessities of life, then what good is that?"— **James 2:15-16**

Inaction is in fact the surest proof that you lie to yourself about the love you think you spread. There is no more powerful driver of action than love.

25

2. Suffering

Frankl believed that purpose was also revealed by the behavior people exhibited while suffering. If you suffer and can't change your circumstances, you may find purpose through the experience of it. Stories of people on their deathbed or those with chronic health problems or those who have lost relatives often describe them finding deep meaning, despite the pain of the journeys being taken.

Most of us won't suffer long enough to long for and find meaning in the experience. But some do. Despite advances in medical technology, we are still helpless against death and some illnesses. And we are often helpless against the destructive behavior of people dear to us. An extreme example is a drug addict who chooses to intoxicate himself, no matter the consequences. Parents or siblings may argue and plead, but people who don't want to change will not do so. And yet … a small number of addicts come out the other side and describe the purpose they discovered.

To find purpose through suffering requires action too. To find meaning in such circumstances, you need to apply a load of mental power to attack your internal demons. You need to answer this question for yourself: *What am I learning through my suffering?*

This mental work requires a lot of focus and effort.

3. Activity

The third way to find purpose is the most common. It's work. Activity. You can find your purpose in what you do: in your career, in your free time, in your work for society or your family.

Random actions won't uncover purpose. Work alone won't help you realize the meaning of your life, as it isn't the work itself that makes you purposeful and happy. Purpose is revealed by the realizations you have *while* you work. If you are stuck in a meaningless job and feel you aren't doing anything of significance, your purpose will not emerge.

Obviously, sitting on the couch watching television is not work, unless you are a program critic. You actually need to move your butt or your mind before you can call it work. And before you can deduce purpose through work, you need to reflect on the value you get from the work and the value you provide.

Almost everyone will find their purpose through work.

To turn an occasional action into a regular commitment needs more than trivial motivation. You need reasons.

You can force yourself to perform some activity once, twice, a couple dozen of times, but without a heartfelt reason to continue, you will give up on it. The force you need to push yourself must be obtained from somewhere. None of us has infinite stores of force. You can argue that sufficient willpower will enable you to do anything. And it's true that willpower can overcome a lot of resistance.

In the year before my final high school exams, I managed to concentrate on my school studies for an hour a day during vacations. Few teenagers will voluntarily do that! But it was only for two months. And I had a powerful reason: I wanted to do well in the exams.

Can you imagine forcing yourself to undertake some activity for decades without a definite motivator? Could you maintain your enthusiasm for a grueling job year after year after year if you had no good reason to do so and could see no definite end to this slog?

I could not.

Let's face it: motivation to do anything eludes us if we have no emotional reason to act. Figures from surveys show that 92% of people who make New Year's resolutions don't follow through.

About half of them give up in the first month. They can't find the motivation to persevere.

Stephen Guise, author of *Mini Habits*, was so frustrated by the elusive nature of motivation, that he abandoned it altogether.

Stephen's problem was the same as those who didn't achieve their New Year's goals. Any discipline undertaken without a driving reason will only be continued while it is convenient, or while you "feel like it." When your reserves of willpower are depleted, you'll quit. That's only natural. Emotions expire. They are temporary in nature. It's impossible for a human being to feel the same level of emotion for an extended period of time. We are just not wired that way. An emotion won't stay the same for longer than a few minutes.

You may say to that … *"Hold on, what about love that endures in a relationship for decades?"* Emotions that last for decades, like love in marriage, need to be constantly worked upon and they constantly change. They transform. Ask anybody who has been married for longer than a couple of years, and you'll find their ways of expressing and feeling love are not the same as they were on their wedding day.

In the end, Stephen decided to instigate very small habits in his life, for which he needed no motivation. His strategy works, to a point. Purpose-driven strategy works better.

When you have a heartfelt purpose, every mission or goal you make towards that end will draw on power within you that isn't available otherwise. And every action you take in alignment with your purpose, like when I write answers to people's questions on a train instead of gazing dreamily out the window, all strengthen and reaffirm your purpose.

Next, we'll look more closely at how you find purpose through work.

Chapter FIVE

Where is the Purpose in Your Work?

I've already referenced Victor Frankl's research and conclusions about purpose. It is a human trait as real and unique as DNA or fingerprints. But it may not be real to *you* yet.

No doubt you've observed successful people following their passions, enjoying a fulfilled life, yet perhaps you can't grasp how to do the same. Those on fire with purpose act like a totally different species. How can they be so convinced about their destiny and committed to its pursuit?

Surely, normal people don't have an intense life purpose? They just live. Or, like Oscar Wilde aptly said: *"They exist."*

However, I invite you to expand your idea of purpose a little. I wrote in *The Art of Persistence:*

"You can just look around, like I am doing this very moment on my daily commute: I notice workers building new track and traffic dispatchers coordinating the trains. I think of the electric lines powering those trains, the people who maintain them, and the train driver who drives the vehicle I'm traveling in.

All are needed. Their coordinated effort makes possible my relatively fast and comfortable daily commute to my job. Thousands of others rely on this team. It's easy to imagine the disaster that could follow if any of these people didn't perform their tasks flawlessly. Intellectually, this is an easy concept to understand. Everyone has a purpose, like each cog in a machine has a place. But does that include me?"

Reflect on that. Does this web include you?

Think about your current job or principal role for a little while. Consider: is this really something you were born to do? How do you feel about that? Dismay?

Unless you are part of the 30% or so who find fulfillment in their work, you may not think you were born to do the work you do at all! It's almost instinctively understandable when you think of relatively unskilled, low-paying jobs like selling burgers. But it's applicable to any kind of role where you don't belong.

I would ask myself this: *"Is restoring databases of test environments in a media company selling people mindless television my life purpose?"* I know my answer; you provide yours for yourself.

It's possible that you feel elation answering this question: *"Yes, I was born to do the job I'm doing! Life is beautiful!"* All in all, 30% is not a small fraction. Three people out of ten are fulfilled in their work.

Is your work aligned with your purpose?

Do you feel comfortable at the thought of spending the rest of your life doing it?

I focus on work because it's the only one of Frankl's three states that seems applicable in my life. I haven't suffered much in my life. It's fairytale-like. I converted from semi-paganism at the age of seventeen. Since then, I consider myself close to God. I met my wife in high school, and we started a family while I was studying at the university. We struggled financially, but got through. I graduated, got a good job, and steadily advanced in my career. We managed to "get ahead." We bought an apartment and a car. I found a calling to become a writer. We bought our first house, my wife's greatest desire. I've now published fourteen books and sold thousands of copies.

The insignificant hardships I've experienced along the way pale against those of someone who struggles with illness and dies of cancer, or loses his child… or was detained in one of the death camps, like Victor Frankl. After the war, he worked to heal the minds and hearts of others who had experienced high levels of suffering. I trust his expertise when he states that pain can be a way to discover the meaning of your life, but I haven't experienced it myself.

I don't feel qualified to talk about love, either. I'm capable of love, but surely not at the heroic level and not as deeply as people who find their meaning in love.

You don't need to be a living saint to find the meaning of your life in love to others. Like with "ordinary" work, you just need to be purposeful about it. All are capable of love, but not many are really able to give their whole life to it.

The number of people I know who I can confidently state live for others could be counted on the fingers of one hand. For example, my neighbor quit her job to take care of her child. She wasn't sour at all. She spent much time outdoors looking after her daughter. She was like a second mother to most of the kids from our apartment block. She was a keen observer of people, too. I learned insights about my own children from her. She was warm and open towards everyone. Her laughter was loud, genuine, and infectious. Yes, I could see her purpose was showing love.

There are people like these all around us. You may be one of them. But if you discover that you spend much of your resources and time on others but regret doing so, then your purpose undoubtedly lies elsewhere. Look to your work to see if you can find it there.

What do you love doing? What would you do even if it didn't pay, if you could somehow survive anyway? Purposeful work is any activity that brings you a sense of fulfillment. It may be a business, it may be work for a non-profit or community organization. You might get fulfillment in being the coach for a school's softball team. It may even be work around your house and garden. It may be scientific research you do as a hobby project.

Whatever it is, "doing it" needs an action on your part. That's why it's called work. It's a four-letter curse to the purposeless, but may be a blessed word to you.

(Chapter SIX)

A Life with Meaning

You may wonder what a purpose-filled life feels like. Let me share a slice of my journey.

I wrote in *The Art of Persistence:*

"After finding my own life purpose, I can compare my experience to that which a baby has while learning to use their hands. Once they discover these amazing tools, they ceaselessly try to master their use. Learning your body's ability is a natural process, but you will not make it any easier for the frustrated infant by trying to explain the function of hands. The strange tentacles must be mastered by trial and error. At first, all seems a mystery, but within a couple of years, there is nothing more natural for a kid than to reach out and grab.

You will experience the same sense of familiarity after you realize your purpose. What seems "out there" right now will feel like part of you, inseparable, once you understand it. Your purpose is part of you in the same way your body is. You can depend on it. It won't abandon you in a least-expected moment."

I wasn't always purposeful. For over 33 years, I lived not knowing the meaning of my life. I know how that feels. For most of us, for most of life, this is "condition normal."

But for me, "normal" was sad and gray. I woke up each morning without anything to look forward to. Most of the time, it was hard to figure out why I should bother getting out of bed. Each day was similar to the previous. The only high points were some family celebrations: birthdays, weddings, etc. My career meant nothing to me. It was just the means to put bread on the table.

Nothing was fulfilling. If I finished a computer game, I soon started another to fill the void. The only happy moments I experienced were those spent playing with my kids. But I had so much else to do in the household, working a full time job and commuting a minimum of 50 minutes one way, that those moments of happiness were rare and short. With each passing month and year, I had less energy to continue in the way I operated.

In order to numb myself against boredom and a lurking sense of helplessness, I filled my time with mindless activities—watching TV, playing computer games, and binge reading.

Now that I have found meaning in my life, my world is different. My life is still full of hardships and struggles. My schedule is even more crowded. I work even harder. My life is getting better, but painfully slowly. My income has grown by 20%, but my wife was unemployed for half a year, so we didn't feel much improvement. I started a writing career, but I still have to work in my day job and I am outside our home twelve hours a day.

But the way I live has totally changed. I wake every day knowing my day will be full of activities that bring me fulfillment. I may not anticipate each day with passion and excitement—no one will feel great every day—but I always know that it will mean something. I spend the first hour charging my batteries—reading, exercising, praying, meditating, learning. On the journey to and from work, I work for myself. I fill my day with a multitude of small disciplines and each of them moves me forward in the areas I choose to master—spirit, health, finance, relationships. I live on purpose.

Getting to that point from my initial mental fog was not instantaneous or easy. It was an uncomfortable process full of stumbles and bruises. Like a baby learning to use her hands, I wasn't easily able to grasp the difficult art of conducting life guided by meaning.

At the beginning, I was only dimly aware that I had such a thing as purpose and I needed to detect it. Then I went through the arduous process of discovering it, like the first attempt of that baby to move her hands in a coordinated fashion.

After that, I experienced a few months of frustration. I got spikes of excitement when I found another piece of my purpose or was able to inch a bit towards fulfilling it, as when the baby discovers she can grab a colorful rattle. Those moments were interspersed with raging frustration when I failed at something I thought would move me forward.

Babies regularly fail at new things, and we all hear their frustrations!

But I tell you, it was all worth it. Can you imagine a kid who got frustrated learning to operate his hands when he was a baby and gave up? What a miserable creature he would be, watching others who were comfortable operating their hands, who could grab whatever they want—that would be torture!

As for learning your purpose, most of the people around you are as miserable as you, so you don't see the difference unless you really search for it. Some individuals have mastered this art and they might make you uncomfortable because of their focus.

Finding your purpose is worth it. You will move from handicapped to proficient. It's not even half as hard as you imagine. In fact, your purpose feels like your skin. After some time you don't think or ruminate about it, you just live with it. It's always there. You can touch it. You can pierce it and then it hurts. It's part of you.

Your purpose is something deeply meaningful, like the work of raising children. If you're driven to fulfill this particular destiny, you'll feel a void in you if you don't do it. Another indication that you've found your true purpose is the realization that this thing is vital to your life. This is how I found writing to be an inseparable part of my purpose.

Writing my first blog helped me at the very beginning to reach out to other people, when I wasn't ready to meet face-to-face with strangers. It was a way to connect with strangers when I couldn't approach them offline. Writing earned me money outside my day job for the first time. That was liberating and stupefying at the same time.

At first, I really didn't believe I could make money from my creative endeavors. I was like an atheist who saw Jesus when the first sales started to trickle in. Writing also allowed me to positively influence the lives of others.

I remember fighting with my wife over my writing in July 2013, less than a couple of months after publishing my first book. I'd been writing for more than half a year and she was exasperated with me. Frankly, I could say little in my defense.

Looking at it logically, I was wasting my time. I had produced, at that time, something like fifty to seventy thousand words, had spent a lot of time and a little bit of money learning how to self-publish, and yet had no results worth mentioning. Not only was the monetary reward negligible, I had received very little reader feedback.

Nonetheless, while I couldn't explain to my wife why I needed to keep writing, I just felt I had to. I was terrified at the thought of abandoning writing; I had found my purpose and I wasn't going to let it go again, just as the baby who has learned to grab a rattle will not let you wrest it from her without a struggle.

When you find your purpose, you just feel it. It may not be logical. It is true nonetheless.

Today, wiser after three further years of experience, I can easily justify my writing to anyone. In December 2013, I received the first of many letters saying that I had changed someone's life for the better. I have now received dozens of them and have a pile of reviews saying the same. I have earned real money. A few thousand dollars from royalties in 2014 allowed us to take a mortgage and buy our first house.

All of this happened because writing IS my thing. But the world doesn't give returns in an instantaneous manner. I felt it was a right path for me, but I needed to work hard for a couple of years to see some results. At the beginning, it's more important what you feel than what you know because you probably know close to nothing.

Today I can look back at my life, examine all the things I've done, and say I was born to write. Finding your purpose will give you the same sense of confidence and stability.

Chapter SEVEN

Finding Your Purpose

I realize I have not given a roadmap yet to finding your purpose because it's not an instruction-manual type of topic. It can't be explained very well without talking about emotions. But I hope you now share my belief that everyone, including you, has a purpose.

And, as you have free will with regard to your purpose, you can do whatever you wish. You can go into denial mode ("I don't have hands" or "OK, I have these tentacles, but I just refuse to use them"), but do you think that attitude will help you find fulfillment?

I recommend you find the purpose for your life and follow your destiny.

If you are still skeptical, wondering if purpose is a fairytale, please suspend your judgment for a little while. At the end of Part One, I'll provide some mental exercises. Please do them first and then turn on your world view again. It won't hurt you, I promise.

It's unlikely anyone ever described Peter Drucker as a mystic. He was one of the greatest managers of the 20th century, a down-to-earth practitioner. He held self-knowledge in very high esteem. He said: *"Success in the knowledge economy comes to those who know themselves—their strengths, their values, and how they best perform."* Drucker came from a practical scientific background yet still considered knowledge about one's strengths and weaknesses crucial to an individual's success.

My world view is totally different than Drucker's. I think God created the world and we are His special creation. I believe He designed the best route for each of us and equipped us with appropriate gifts to follow this route.

In the end, the conclusion is the same, however. Not knowing yourself, and not playing on your strengths, is like having a car with a manual transmission that you always drive in first gear. Regardless of your beliefs about where talents and strengths come from, please accept that we all have a "sweet spot" and do whatever you can to identify it.

Finding the meaning of your life is, in my experience, a grueling job. You examine yourself bit by bit and try to make a nice picture with the puzzle pieces you get from your answers. Of course, you could sit and wait for instant enlightenment. It happens. (People win lotteries too.)

Saint Paul had it easy. He didn't have to walk three years by Jesus' side or watch him dying. He was happily occupied with his own business (mayhem and murders) when, literally out of the blue, a light dawned on him, and he radically changed his life from that very moment.

"Only three things will change behavior in the long term. Option A. Have an epiphany [...]
Creating an epiphany is difficult. You should rule out Option A unless you have mystical powers."— BJ Fogg, PhD, Director of Persuasive Tech Lab at Stanford University

In the media, you don't hear about the millions of lottery losers. For each lucky guy there are millions less lucky. For each person who was suddenly enlightened there are millions who aren't.

You don't have to wait in desperation for the intervention of a higher power into your life to find your purpose. After reading *The Slight Edge,* I was able to create a personal mission statement defining the meaning of my life in about three months. I definitely had a moment of enlightenment, but it took me some time to realize what it all meant.

While creating my mission statement, I mainly used *The 7 Habits of Highly Effective People.* Although that book was designed to help individuals boost their productivity, the section that gave guidance on how to search for your life's meaning was very helpful. In my view, that's part of the reason why the book is still so wildly popular.

The 7 Habits ... was published for the first time in 1988, but it is still occupying bestseller ranks on Amazon. The popularity of the personal mission statement concept is proof enough for me that gradual enlightenment is possible. I later wrote a guide titled *A Personal Mission Statement: Your Road Map to Happiness*; it has sold well. This suggests that more and more people are choosing this path for getting to know themselves better.

"Pray as if everything depends on God, work as if everything depends on you." — **Saint Augustine**

I advise praying to God for enlightenment, while simultaneously working on it by yourself.

How should you begin?

If you are lucky enough to have access to external sources of wisdom, I recommend you start there. I am referring to supportive friends or family, the kind that will be brutally honest with you. Interview them about your behavior and traits. Ask what they admire in you and what they despise; ask how they perceive you; ask what they think are your strengths and weaknesses.

In our current era, many of us are bereft of deep and meaningful relationships, sadly. I was in that situation when I started my soul searching. My best friends were living hundreds of miles away and my wife wasn't actively supporting my personal development.

If this is your reality too, there are tools you can use to get some of the same information you'd get from friends and family. I don't think they are as effective, mainly because of a human's tendency for self-deceit. You and I both tend to overestimate our good traits and underestimate the bad ones when evaluating ourselves. However, you can try a few such tools and look for repeating patterns.

In the autumn of 2012, I was involved in a recruiting process for a Scandinavian company and a part of it was a personality test. I also signed up to Tony Robbins' email list and as a free gift I was provided with a DISC® personality test. The results of both tests gave me a lot of material to ponder, and I could compare them. I repeated the DISC test a year later with similar results.

The people who designed these tests were aware of our inclination to deceive ourselves and did a good job of removing our rose-colored glasses. The results may not completely define who and how you are, but if your take the process seriously, you'll get good material.

There is also a strength finder test. I've never taken it, but it's highly recommended by a few people I respect.

I didn't use any of the test results as the frame for my Personal Mission Statement, but these days, my lifestyle and path are being constantly appraised by many, through my writing. And the feedback I get indicates that my readers find my strengths to lie where the test results indicated.

Whatever methods you choose for finding the meaning of your life, remember that this process is not instantaneous and involves your whole person. It's not enough to think hard about it. You need to involve your emotions too. The best way to do that is to employ your imagination and put it in overdrive.

I seriously advise you to write down both your ruminations and your feelings after self-discovery sessions. Don't just keep your thoughts in your head. The act of writing them down will both clarify them and solidify them in your memory.

Exercises

I hope you've read my book *Know Yourself Like Your Success Depends on It*; if not, this is the perfect moment to do so. One thing is sure—after you do these exercises, you will know yourself better. And this knowledge is the most precious gift you can ever get.

To begin, I suggest an exercise from *7 Habits of Highly Successful People* that helped me greatly in creating my mission statement. It is a perfect tool for detecting your purpose. I encourage you to do it right now (or whenever you have a spare five minutes).

Don't postpone it until tomorrow; I urge you to do it today before you go to sleep.

Close your eyes and imagine your funeral. Imagine who is there. Imagine people giving their speeches about you. What would you like to hear from your spouse, your children, coworkers, employees, neighbors, your brothers and sisters of the same

43

religion, relatives? "Listen" to a few such speeches in your head and then take a pen and paper and write down your eulogy. Write down what would you like people to say about you when you are gone.

Part II
Discovering Your Compass

Chapter EIGHT

Defining Your Vision

Even as a "zombie," I had a dream. I've been living with this dream since I got involved in the church community, back in 1996. Nonetheless, after diligently attending meetings for more than fifteen years, I had been disappointed by my progress. Clearly, the path I was following wasn't quite right. I needed to try something new. This realization was the underlying reason for my transformation.

I knew the oft-used definition of insanity: *"Doing the same over again and expecting different results."* I was subconsciously looking for alternative routes. And once I admitted to myself the unlikelihood of ever realizing my vision, I also opened a door in my mind that led to new places.

The moral of my story is this: having a vision for your life always helps.

I had a completely ordinary life, indistinguishable from that of millions of other city dwellers. Naturally, I wanted wealth, happiness, and fame like any other man. I hadn't yet realized those wishes, so life was frustrating. The new toys I wanted were out of reach.

But new toys weren't at the top of my list. I had one special thing; I had my dream, a compass in my hand that always pointed north. This "one special thing" gnawed at my conscience, a constant presence in my heart. My vision never allowed me to fully immerse myself in the superficial pleasures of daily life. Deep inside, I always strove for more.

No matter how helpless you seem to be, or how hopeless your

vision seems to people around you, your purpose is the compass that will keep your life on track.

Creating a Vision for Your Life

Why not create a grand and lofty vision for your life?

Without a vision burning in you, you'll need to be superhuman to be able to focus on current tasks without slipping into ruminations about either the past or the future. There are people who can do it—monks, top sportsmen, and other top performers. However, to get to that point they usually need to train for years.

It's also very likely they have some kind of vision that drives them through the countless hours of practice.

You've probably heard the saying, "Start with the end in mind." Many of those who learn about this concept miss the significance of the first word. Certainly, the last bit, "… end in mind" is important too; I have a lot of thoughts to offer you about that. However, nothing in your mind will help you get things achieved if you don't *start*.

You may have goals and a beautiful personal mission statement. You may take time to recite long prayers and spend hours composing and looking at a vision board. But these preparatory steps are in vain without action. No amount of "end" in your mind will help you if you don't take the first step. And the next step.

If you can mobilize yourself to do something now that will bring you closer to achieving your dreams, you are a tiny bit closer to reaching them. And as you will most likely live for decades, "now" is a very short period of time. You need to link together countless "now" moments to get significant results. Your vision is the medium that connects those moments.

There are a few instances of people starting ventures without much thinking and making successes out of them. Usually though, when we start something, we mostly fail. That's natural. At the beginning of any new path, your experience is nil; your skills are undeveloped.

As you begin, fame and wealth are still a long way off. And an ordinary person doesn't like change, so your biggest risk in a new venture is that you'll fail to achieve any—because our natural behavior is to avoid it. Change brings a risk of failure and humiliation.

As it tries to avoid change, your mind will play tricks. It will self-sabotage, self-criticize, make you complacent... these are some of the filters your brain has inherited or established to help you survive.

What are these filters? For one, your brain is constantly on the lookout for danger. We are wired to fear loud noises. This is a basic filter. Every other impulse gets ignored if a sudden noise is registered. Our "fight or flight or freeze" reaction is triggered in that situation.

Filters also affect our deep beliefs and social interactions. You react to every perceived danger to your mental integrity or social status. You do it without thinking; this is how your mind works. And that's why you need a vision. This is a filter that you consciously control. It acts as a lens to help you focus on the things that matter.

I'm not the only voice advocating the importance of vision.

The interesting thing about concepts like *end in mind, vision, purpose, life's passion,* or *have big goals* is that virtually every teacher of success advises arming yourself with one kind or

49

another. If you've studied personal development at any length, you'll realize there's a constant battle of opinions: *set goals, no, never set goals; start small, no, start big; use affirmations, no don't use affirmations as they are the beginning of illusion; think, no: act.*

This range of opinions about the "right way" is natural; we all have different experiences and perspectives. Nonetheless, there is no debate over the importance of vision. All teachers stress the importance of it in one way or another.

Stephen R. Covey popularized the personal mission statement. Jim Rohn was a fan of setting goals, including long-term goals that took decades to accomplish. Peter Drucker recommended setting goals too, but no further ahead than two to three years because he felt continually changing conditions meant longer-term goals weren't meaningful.

Wallace D. Wattles used the word vision. Earl Nightingale, in his famous *The Strangest Secret*, compared a man without purpose to a ship without rudder or crew and asked: *"What chances has this ship to reach its destination?"*

Since EVERYBODY agrees it's important, there has to be something in it, don't you think?

The easiest way to begin developing your vision is through visualization. This is simply the use of your imagination. Everybody has it in some stage of development because we think in images. Whenever a thought occurs in your mind, an image will flash through your head.

Napoleon Hill explains in *Think and Grow Rich* how he created a mastermind group of famous people in his imagination. Maxwell Maltz, the author of *Psycho-Cybernetics*, advises the extensive use of imagination exercises to modify your self-image. Victor Frankl, founder of the Logotherapy psychology school, spent hours and hours inside his head while imprisoned in the German death camp, imagining interactions with his wife and scenes from normal life.

Top sport performers use visualizations to stay at the top. In *The Power of Habit*, there is a story about Michael Phelps, the best swimmer in the history of the world. At the Olympics in Beijing, he won six gold medals. During one of the races in that competition, his goggles punctured and he was forced to swim practically blind. But after visualizing his performance so many times, it made no difference for him. He won anyway.

I know it's hard to put your trust in such an intangible thing. I was in your shoes. I actually thought I'd go mad if I tried to visualize a better future that didn't exist yet. And my imagination is relatively poor. The images in my head are static, monochromatic, and fuzzy. I can feel emotions easier than I can picture images. So I was reluctant to use visualization, until I studied personal development further and learned that almost everyone agrees about its usefulness.

When I thought some more, I had to admit two things. Firstly, my life wasn't that great and I wanted to change it. Secondly, the people who recommended visualization had more success than me; they probably knew what they were talking about. If it was good enough for saints, bestselling authors, and sportsmen, surely it had to be good for me too.

A final thought on this—as you know, I'm fascinated by saints. I was amazed to discover that Saint Ignatius Loyola's famous

Spiritual Exercises were based on using imagination. Other saints advocated and practiced the same. I found diaries, journals, and autobiographies with descriptions of them exercising their imaginations to connect with God.

I realized that my reflections on the Passion of Christ needed the use of my imagination to connect with Him in those moments.

It's impossible to blindly stumble upon success. Ask every successful person about their journey. No one will answer: *"Well, I just kind of wandered along doing the next step and then another one, and suddenly I finished at this place of great success."*

Without a vision, even apparently good fortune—like winning a lottery—can turn into disaster, as shown by the fate of many lottery winners. We are wired for growth and direction. When we wander, we get frustrated and tired relatively fast. When you have an end in mind, you can run or crawl for miles.

(Chapter NINE)

Your Personal Philosophy

I'm sure you understand now that it's important to have a vision.
But how can you create and pursue it in your life? If you are
purposeless, you won't have any idea where to start and even
fewer ideas on how to proceed further. In my experience, vision
and purpose are to be detected rather than created. They are
intimately yours, so looking for them in the outside world will be
unsuccessful. You need to make them part of your constitution to
be able to use them.

*"It's the filter for everything you encounter and the generator of
everything you do. It's your sanity shield and action engine." -*
Trickle Down Mindset

The most basic part of you is your personal philosophy. It
determines which external impulses will be filtered out and which
will be allowed into your conscious mind. Your vision must be a
part of your filtering mechanism, or the useful pieces of reality, the
ones that could be contributing to the realization of your purpose,
will simply get ignored. Your personal philosophy is formed by
three main factors: your internal dialog, your data sources, and the
people you interact with. All three must be congruent with your
vision to solidify the right personal philosophy.

In order to make my vision real, I pray a lot and closely scrutinize
my thoughts (internal dialog). I also study the Bible and read from
a book written by one of the saints every day (data sources). I'm
also an active member of a church community (people).

Your self-image is the result of your personal philosophy. You can
reverse-influence your philosophy by affecting your self-image. If

you want to get a deep knowledge on how to mold your self-image, I recommend *Psycho-Cybernetics* by Maxwell Maltz.

The important takeaway from Maltz's book is that your self-image is the foundation of every behavior. Every sentence of the kind: "I'm a person who…" literally can't be opposed by your subconscious. If you think about yourself as a diligent person, you will act with diligence. If you think you are shy, you will be timid in relationship with strangers. You just can't help that.

The best remedy for negative beliefs about yourself is awareness and conscious counteraction. But you'll need to do it consistently and regularly. Any activities intended to improve your personal philosophy or change your self-image should be performed daily.

"You become what you think about all day long." — **Ralph Waldo Emerson**

"You become what you do most of the time." — **Anthony Robbins**

Your goal is to be immersed in this new mindset of yours. It can't be done by practicing some activities once a week or once a month. You have to incorporate such activities into every day. If you want to affect your personal philosophy, introduce some daily disciplines that involve absorbing data, doing self-analysis, or interacting with people.

You can mingle these. For example, interacting in an online community can be both a data source and a way to meet people who enforce your new point of view. If you want to rebuild your self-image, visualize yourself acting in a new way, every day, and build habits that will support this new view of yourself.

Take it slowly; there's more chance of success. If you are shy, don't try to reach out to all the attractive people you see tomorrow to convince yourself that you are bold and confident. Just inch yourself each day in the right direction. And ensure your affirmations, visualizations, and deeds are congruent. I don't think I can stress this enough.

When I began overcoming my shyness, I started by looking other people in the eyes. Then I added a tiny discipline of smiling at them. After a few months of constant practice, I was good enough to approach strangers, open my mouth, and utter words.

The key here was daily practice. I couldn't get 1% better every day by practicing just once a week. I couldn't develop an *"I'm progressing"* mindset if I didn't do at least a little every day.

A personal mission statement is your life's compass. It's not a GPS. A personal mission statement shows the general direction of your life, but doesn't provide specific routes. It works powerfully; I've experienced it.

I have lofty dreams. I want to change the world. But even now I have no idea how to do this. I am hesitant about the course I should take. However, my personal mission statement works perfectly; it keeps me aligned with my values.

Whenever I skew from the True North of my life, I immediately sense it. That was the case with the Kindle Gold Rush program I decided to try at the end of 2013. Within a couple of weeks, I had watched the training videos and interacted in the group's forum, and I could see the business potential.

But intuitively I knew it was not the way I should go. Pursuing that path would have been—for me—like this phrase from the Bible: *"What, then, will anyone gain by winning the whole world and forfeiting his life?"* — **Matthew 16: 26a**

Two years later, I'm not much closer to reaching my financial goals, but I have experienced so many amazing moments on the path that are in line with my True North that I don't regret following it for a moment.

I have connected closely with many readers and have received amazing feedback. I'm stoked I chose this path. When I hear about readers having wins—saying that they lost weight and improved their health; that they developed their mission statements and changed their direction in life; that they found their inner strength to stay consistent with the small habits steadily improving their lives—the news is worth so much more to me than all the money in the world.

While creating your mission statement, do so with the intent that it will serve you for the rest of your life. Depending on your age and health, this may be a while. And while developing it, my suggestion is not to focus on the things you want to possess, see, or experience. Instead, focus more on the kind of person you want to become.

You may want to be a saint, a millionaire, or a person who overcomes racism or hunger for good. Of course, right now you are not. And you have only a very dim idea how to transform from who you are now to who you want to be. It doesn't matter much. You need a compass, not a GPS.

Keep your personal mission statement in the present tense and use positive sentences. (Avoid "don'ts," as in sentences like "I don't watch TV!"). Brian Tracy says that our subconscious mind absorbs messages much better when they are written positively. I trust he did his homework.

I used some negative statements in my original mission statement and noticed that they weren't as effective as I would have wished them to be. I tweaked them, with good results. My experience says that positive sentences are better.

"There is nothing wrong with affirmations, provided what you are affirming is the truth." — **Jim Rohn**

Keep in mind that your mission statement must be grounded in reality. The more "fantasy-like" it is, the more resistance you'll face from your subconscious mind. People often give up on affirmations because they think they don't work, but they are much more likely to work if they are realistic.

For example, when I was creating my personal mission statement I wrote, *"I'm becoming a writer."* At that time, I hadn't published a single word. I had a desire to become a writer, but not much more. That statement was acceptable for me. It was true. I was in the process of becoming a writer.

More than a year later, when I had over a dozen blog posts up and five e-books published—the last one an Amazon bestseller—I modified this sentence into: "I'm a writer." In my new circumstances, it rang true in my ears.

Chapter TEN

Using Your Personal Mission Statement

The real value of your personal mission statement lies not in the process of creation, no matter how much you learn about yourself during this period, but in putting your mission statement to use. If you don't use it every day, it will become like a printed certificate of accomplishment on the wall: possibly impressive when completed, but less and less relevant as time goes on.

You will have noticed that I have already emphasized several times the importance of daily work. And the best way to do anything on a daily basis is to develop a habit. Make a habit of reviewing or reflecting on your mission statement every day.

There are a multitude of methods to review your mission statement. You can read it, you can repeat it (or fragments of it) in your mind, you can record it on audio or video and listen to/watch it, you can create a vision board based on it. Whatever you choose to do, make sure you do it every day.

I repeat my verbose personal mission statement in my mind every morning while preparing to work or during chores when I have days off. Each morning I also look at my vision board, which is based on my mission statement. That's two iron habits. The trigger to the first one is opening my eyes when I wake up. The trigger to the second one is finishing another of my daily habits.

After a workout, I drink a glass of water and turn on my computer. Then I sit in front of it and play my vision board. I have my mission statement recorded on audio and I listen to it from time to time, when I feel like it. Very rarely do I read my personal mission statement.

Your preferences may be totally different. Only one thing is important: choose the method that serves you, that helps you, and then stick to your routine. As long as you refer to your personal mission statement daily, you are fine. If you can't keep your routine, if distractions or circumstances cause you to miss doing it every few days, then change your method. Tune it till you find the perfect one for you.

The methods I mentioned above are just a baseline. Absorbing your mission statement is one thing, but it is given to you to live it. You can encounter an everyday situation that will be somehow relevant to your mission and ruminate about it. I wrote pretty specific things in my statement like *"I smile at strangers"* or *"I hug my kids."* Those everyday acts gave me a pause and a second of reflection on my mission when I performed them. Everything you put a conscious effort into will result in better results than anything done with mindless execution.

But your resources, attention, time, and willpower are finite. Automated actions need much less focus and still provide results. Feed your subconscious with your mission and it will find a way to realize it. I found this way less frustrating than goal setting.

When you set a goal, you need to devise and follow some plan to reach it. You need a deadline. You need metrics. Inevitably, you will miss some of them. Then the frustration kicks in and usually ruins your plans. You are trying to compensate, to do too much too quickly, and fail even sooner and harder. Or you simply quit and feel no joy in pursuing the goal you seem to be unable to reach.

Chapter ELEVEN

Follow Your Compass

Four years ago I hadn't even dreamed about writing. Even after I had decided I wanted to write and developed my personal mission statement, I had no idea how I would fulfill its words. I just repeated them every day for weeks and months. I got some ideas and tried them.

My first blog was far from being a success. My first short fiction story wasn't greeted with much appreciation. My second blog was a ghost town. Every day I published a short post and nobody read them. My third blog wasn't much better.

Only after all those failures did I try publishing on Kindle. Fast-forward to nine months after I published my first book and bam! I was a writer.

A personal mission statement shows you direction, but doesn't give you directions. You just look at the compass and figure out which route to take. And you shouldn't worry about how things will happen. If you are not some crazy genius, you won't know anyway.

What's the use of agonizing over it? Your job is not figuring out "how" when you have no clue. Your job is to look at the compass and decide which route is more likely to bring you closer to your destination. At the beginning of your journey, your main job is to refer to your mission statement every day. Show up consistently and the events will unfold.

This is of ultimate importance because your mind will try to trick you out of showing up. Your subconscious mind is powerful. There is an analogy between the subconscious and conscious, wherein the first is illustrated as an elephant and the second as is its rider. The rider can steer the animal using the power of his muscles and reins… for a limited period of time. Then he will fatigue and the animal will go where it wants.

Sometimes it can seem like your subconscious isn't an elephant but a herd of large dinosaurs. Luckily, your ability to influence your subconscious is actually quite close to the ability of the elephant's rider. You have a chance.

Your subconscious will try to steer you away from your personal mission statement. Its main goal is to preserve your energy. Following your mission consumes a lot of energy. Steering you away from your mission is the easiest, least energy consuming way to maintain the status quo, to avoid change.

Refer to your personal mission statement every day. Read it, watch it, listen to it, recite it. You have power over your actions. Going back to my example, I had next to no power over people who browsed Amazon looking for books to read. I couldn't coerce them to buy and read my books.

Back when I composed my personal mission statement, I hadn't even heard about Amazon. I had no clue how to become a writer. But this one thing I could do: I could read my personal mission statement every day. And I did.

When your subconscious mind faces such stubbornness, it has three choices: ignore your mission, go crazy, or submit to your will. You've already taken away the easiest one—ignoring the matter of your mission.

I suppose it's possible you will go crazy, in theory. Your subconscious can't stand cognitive dissonance, observing one thing and believing another. It can't stand you saying that you are a painter, while realizing you never paint, so it might invent stories to justify the incompatibility you're displaying.

Luckily, the more common option taken is to submit to your will. Your subconscious will start to look for ways to fulfill your mission. It will adjust its filters looking for opportunities to make your crazy dream come true.

Instead of Exercises

If you feel like writing your personal mission statement, I have a gift for you, currently the best resource in the world in this area, my book A Personal Mission Statement: Your Road Map to Happiness.

Visit ExpandBeyondYourself.com/pms provide your best email and you will get a Kindle or audio version (or both if you wish) of the book. Once again, its:

ExpandBeyondYourself.com/pms

Part III
The Nature of Motivation

Chapter TWELVE

Extrinsic Motivation

You may wonder how a personal mission statement will motivate you to stay committed to a single direction when distractions and attractions lie on every side, and life itself constantly changes the nature of the challenges we face.

Consider what motivates most people. Most of us get excited by one of two things, or both: stuff and significance. We like toys and we like power or influence. You're probably roused to work for one of these whenever conditions present you with an opportunity.

But reflect: motivation of this kind is temporary, external. It is powerful when it works, but it doesn't come from inside you, it is given to you on a silver plate. It's not yours.

It can be ignited by your senses—you see a gorgeous specimen of the opposite sex and feel aroused, you hear someone talking about getting rich quickly and you get excited, and so on. But once the external igniter fades, your emotions quieten down. You can no longer tap into that external source of power.

So, is it totally useless? Not exactly. Extrinsic motivation is a great igniter. It is perfect to get you started, but not much use to keep you going. I found a wonderful analogy of it in the science fiction series *Troy Rising*. The humanity threatened by the aliens developed a space propulsion system utilizing nuclear weapons. A giant cosmic station was propelled by a series of nuclear explosions. To protect the station from being destroyed by them, a force shield was employed.

That's what utilizing extrinsic motivation for continuous progress looks like. You need explosion after explosion of strong emotion to keep you going. Afterwards, without the thrill of strong emotions, you feel exhaustion and emptiness. You need to shield yourself from the destructive effects of such explosions.

They are some people who harness nuclear-like strong emotions and seem to be always hyped. I admire them, but I'm not one of them, and I can't teach you this art. I harnessed this power to start me in the right direction, but I quickly switched to using mundane, emotionless habits to keep me in motion.

Chapter THIRTEEN

Will the Appeal of Power or Possessions Motivate You?

The biggest threat in using external motivations, those shiny objects that fire up your imagination and emotions, is that you can actually get what you want. The sad reality? No external object, or promotion, can satisfy your internal hunger for higher achievement.

You'll feel good about getting what you wanted … for a short time. Then you'll need an even stronger stimulus to continue your journey. Achieving the next goal will only repeat that cycle and, in the end, you will realize that this road leads nowhere. You cannot possess the whole world.

So, the smart way of using shiny objects is to keep them constantly in front of you without ever (or very rarely) actually getting them. That's the real function of vision boards full of fabulous cars, beautiful houses, and tropical beaches.

A vision board is there to fire up your imagination and make you move your butt. If you actually win everything shown in your pictures—and stop looking for more—you will stop your efforts. Why should you hustle if you have everything you've ever wanted?

One of my heroes, entrepreneur Pat Flynn, uses exactly this mechanism to give himself a surge of motivation. When starting his business, he hung a picture of sport car—a Lamborghini—to have something to aim at. Nowadays he is making around

$100,000 a month, so he could afford this car. Be he is wise enough to know that getting this fancy toy wouldn't do him much good. He would have been satisfied for a finite amount of time, but his drive would have gone.

Now he has another kind of a vision board—a corkboard full of thank you notes from the people he helped. It's more intrinsic motivation but presented in a visible form.

Extrinsic motivation is not dependable. Paradoxically, getting what you want makes you miserable and divests you of a drive. Analyze it. We were talking about satisfaction among the workforce. Why do most people go and do their jobs? For the paycheck of course. A paycheck is external motivation. How many people would still work if they didn't get money for doing so? Do you know anyone who was fired but kept coming to work because he just loved it? That's exactly how extrinsic motivation works. The moment it's gone is the moment you stop right where you are.

There is a better kind of motivation —an intrinsic one. It comes from within and you have total control over it. You can fire it up or turn it down, like the driver can regulate a steam engine. It acts like a pull, not a push. How so? Because YOU are the only entity in the universe you really control.

Anything else—things, approval, recognition from peers or family, the weather, and so on—is external and not really controllable by you. That's why people driven by extrinsic motivation are not in control of their lives.

Here's an illustration of different motivations:

Right now, I work two jobs. One is my day job. I do it to earn a living. As soon as this extrinsic motivation disappears, I'm gone from there. No paycheck means no Michal behind the desk.

My other job is my writing. Here's how my writing career began: I wrote my first book in April and May 2013. I published it on 26th of May 2013. My second book was published in July 2013. In August, I also published a public domain book with a personal tweak.

In the following three months I wrote a booklet about learning speed reading, a Polish-language philosophy work on Catholic Church teachings about progress (it is still in my drawer), and a time management book for busy ordinary mortals. Each of those works was written, proofread, rewritten, and edited. Each meant at least 100 precious hours taken out of my life.

At the end of October 2013, I had three titles on sale. Do you know how many copies I sold in just over five months? I sold one hundred and forty five. Do you know how much money I made in that period? I made eleven euros, less than two cents per hour.

You might think I was getting other things. Well, I *was,* but I wasn't getting anything material—no presents, favors, publicity, job offers, or anything else. Yet I didn't stop writing. I never lost my motivation to do so. What was motivating me; what was I getting?

Writing was something I felt I had to do. It was something I identified myself with. I wanted to be a writer. Writers write. I was writing. And I didn't receive any significant money from my writing for thirteen months after I wrote the first word for my first book.

My motivation wasn't grounded in the number of sales or amount of recognition I got. It was grounded in my self-image. Writers write. I was literally unable to stop writing. This was intrinsic motivation at work. This is the motivation you need to find.

I see intrinsic motivation coming from the deeper part of human nature. It doesn't come from the same place your personal wants and wishes come. Everybody wants to be healthy, rich, happy, peaceful, recognized, important, and loved.

But not many people achieve anything from this list. A very few have it all at once. Simply wanting to fulfill your personal dreams doesn't cut the mustard. It won't drive you forward far enough, or for long enough. In the end, these things only appear to supply extrinsic motivation.

The difference between those who achieve their dreams and those who are still just dreamers lies in their motivation. Those who accomplish a lot don't just serve themselves, they serve the multitude. That's why they succeed. They utilize the basic economy law articulated by Zig Ziglar: *"You will get all you want in life, if you help enough other people get what they want."*

This phenomenon is a bit similar to the difference between adolescents and adults. Both groups have basically the same abilities. Are you so much different now than you were at fifteen or seventeen? My body was in a similar shape, my mind quite as sharp as well. And today's youth-worshipping culture claims that adolescents have stronger and healthier bodies and are learning faster.

But 99% of young people are dependent on their parents, not the other way around. Why is that so? In his audio program *Cultivating the Unshakable Character*, Jim Rohn defined the difference very aptly. An adolescent's attitude is, "Leave me alone! I'll take care of my needs." The adult's attitude is: "I'll take care of you. You can depend on me."

To find the powerful sources of intrinsic motivation you must possess that attitude when pursuing your dreams. Simply put, you must serve others, so they can depend on you.

Chapter FOURTEEN

Will the Passion for Others Motivate You?

Where else could you find motivation to follow the path of your personal mission statement? Who do you know, or know of, who might inspire you? There are four main groups of people who can motivate you better than you do it yourself.

1. Your peers.

Do you know the best motivation for a soldier under fire? When in action, a soldier doesn't think about honors, medals, or how good his deeds will look in the papers. He acts because his mates expect it of him. Of course, I got this knowledge not by being under fire but from reading science fiction books written by ex-soldiers and reading soldiers' biographies.

I believe it, because every single man who has ever been under fire says the same thing: if he acted at all, he acted with the thought that his peers counted on him.

You don't need to go to war to utilize this kind of motivation. You just need someone that counts on you. I started a mini-mastermind group with my two good friends last year. We make a call every week, summarize our past week, and set goals for one another.

One Friday evening I was preparing myself for the next such call. I reviewed my weekly goals and I felt ashamed that at least half of what I had planned had been barely touched. I didn't want to report my activities with so much undone, so I decided to do a thing I'd procrastinated about for a month or two.

This involved recording seven questions for my mentor's podcast. I don't have proper recording equipment and the internal microphone in my laptop provides awful sound quality, so I did the recordings on my mobile. It took a while. My far-from-perfect spoken English meant I needed to shoot every recording at least twice before I got it more or less right.

As I have no idea how to record sound only, I recorded video. Then I connected the mobile to my laptop, chose the files with the actual questions, and discarded the failed attempts. I converted the files to MP3 format, put them in a single zip file, and uploaded it at my site. Finally, I wrote an email to my mentor.

All this took about an hour of my Friday evening, and I was motivated to finally do it because I was ashamed of appearing in front of my accountability partners with empty hands.

2. Your mentors.

It's almost certain you have people in your life you respect immensely. These could be people close to you, such as your father or grandma, your manager in your first job, or your coach. Regardless of who they are, you'll naturally want to earn their respect.

You may not have a mentor right now. Not everybody is blessed to be in relationship with a mentor who supervises them closely and personally, but this kind of connection seems to work well if you are pursuing success. Many successful people experienced breakthroughs because of a mentor's intervention at some moment in their lives. Jim Rohn had Earl Shoaff; Bob Proctor met his mentor when he was broke and without any bright prospect for his future. I could mention hundreds of other such stories.

But your mentor doesn't have to be close to you. He doesn't even have to be living.

Jim Rohn knew his mentor for only about five years before he died. However, every time Jim spoke about being motivated by the relationship with his mentor, he insisted that even many years after Earl's death, he still considered what his mentor would have thought about his actions.

I have a similar story. I listened to Jim for the first time in 2012, three years after his death. But I tell you, I wouldn't have had him disappointed in me. I name myself his student and I try to act as I imagine he would advise.

3. Your family.

Our need for love is the most basic human need. There has been research done in the past comparing kids in orphanages who received emotionless physical care and kids raised in foster families. Kids in orphanages were fed and clothed. They were bathed and obviously had a place to live and feel secure. But it all was done with few hugs and smiles and little encouragement. The results of such experiments were always the same. Kids from orphanages died in higher numbers than kids in foster families. Those who survived also had worse health than their peers raised with love.

The most vivid results were when kids from orphanages were compared to kids raised in a prison by their own incarcerated mothers. Kids from prisons had better results in every area: they were healthier, self-confident, and learned faster.

Do you want to earn the respect and love of your relatives? Of course you do. All humans do, on some level. Use this natural urge as a motivator. It will take you further than just the dreams of a comfortable life, freedom, or journeys.

In *Cultivating the Unshakable Character*, Jim Rohn told a story of a young man who wanted to take his family for one-year trip around the world to provide them with experiences and memories for a lifetime. After a seminar, he approached Jim Rohn and asked him for advice on how to earn enough money to afford this trip. Mr. Rohn was impressed by the level of his motivation and passion. He reported:

"There were literally tears in his eyes as he said this, and although I haven't heard from him since then, I have no doubt that he will achieve his goal. In my mind's eye, I could picture him over the coming years, working long hours, meeting deadlines, overcoming obstacles, doing everything it takes to be successful—and doing it gladly! After all, he was motivated by something more than the simple desire for financial success and the material rewards that come with it. This man was working hard because he desired to give his wife and children a lifetime's worth of priceless memories."

4. The whole human family.

I truly believe that those who achieve the most in this world are motivated by a desire to serve "the human family," those outside their normal circle of acquaintance. A British anthropologist, Dunbar, discovered than we can have close relationships with only about 100 to 250 people. We tend to treat people outside this circle as alien in some way, possibly dangerous.

But some people reach out outside this circle of 250 and connect more widely. They work for the advancement of all and they serve as many people as they can. People such as Martin Luther King, Nelson Mandela, Mother Teresa, John Paul II, Ronald Reagan, and Mahatma Gandhi were driven by more than a desire to serve or impress just their family or mentors. They also reaped a proportionate reward. If you need a huge vision to drive you, as they did, you too should aim for saving the world.

As I've said, you don't have to go full-scale right away. You don't (and most of us just cannot) become a saint overnight. For example, you might not be able to ameliorate hunger in the whole world, but you can do something for the homeless in your district. Or you could develop your business so you can help finance research for the cure for cancer.

My mother jokingly refers to my father as Father Teresa from Greenwich because he just can't sit on his hands when others need his help. She thinks his benevolence is abused. Dad admits the possibility, but it doesn't stop him from helping out whenever he can.

I have a similar streak. The idea of assisting peers or family doesn't motivate me much. But when I finally realized that I might, through writing, help a bigger number of people and simultaneously take better care of my family, there was no power that could stop me. I took massive action and kept going for weeks, months, and years writing my books.

Find your own level and stick to it. Examine your past and determine which kind of social environment makes you to take action.

Exercises

Think about the people you know well (your best mate from childhood, your grandmother, your brother, your spouse, etc.). Which of these are likely to tell you the truth as they see it?

Talk to them. Ask them questions about your behavior, strengths, and skills. Ask *why* they see a certain trait or skill in you. And ask for your weaknesses to be identified.

Write down the answers. Reflect. Compare the answers of one with another. Which are true for you?

Part IV
Keeping Focus in Your Life

Chapter FIFTEEN

Lens for Focus

Your life's overall vision and direction should be outlined in your personal mission statement. And to get the best use out of it, you'll need to set your internal filters for this one thing. You need some kind of tool that will serve you as the lens of your focus.

There are a multitude of tools available: affirmations, vision boards, written goals, prayer, journaling, meditations, and more. Any of these will help you focus your attention and activity. However, whatever focusing methods you choose, ensure you can maintain them.

I would have probably gone crazy if I'd tried using goal setting as a lens for my focus. When I dedicate my effort to attaining a goal, I can easily dedicate too much energy to achieving deadlines and milestones. I tend to beat myself up when I don't reach these markers, which happens all the time.

You don't have to restrict yourself to only a single method. When I started my transformation, I was so desperate that I tried almost everything at once and I've stuck with most of them. I just don't want to miss any chance for significant progress.

However, even manic me built those activities gradually. I started by simply repeating my personal mission statement and then added a vision board based on it. Later, I introduced daily journaling and gradually expanded its scope. I also increased the time of my daily prayer and introduced meditation into my days. All of the above I found easy to do in short bursts. As you can see, you are not limited by one single method.

Chapter SIXTEEN

Will Goal Setting Help Your Focus?

What is a goal? One definition says: *'the result or achievement toward which effort is directed; aim; end.'* The business dictionary says it is *'An observable and measurable end result having one or more objectives to be achieved within a more or less fixed timeframe.'*

The etymology of this word is unclear. When in use around 1530, it meant *'end point of race.'* The word appears once before in an early 14th century poem meaning *'boundary, limit.'* A sport sense and a figurative sense of this word are attested from as early as the 1540s.

Some people really like working with goals and others don't. Let's take a look at both sides of the coin to help you decide which method will work best for you.

A Goal-less Approach

I suck at reaching my goals. I'm great at setting them but achieving them is a totally different story. This has given me an incredible amount of frustration and disappointment with the goal-setting idea. My problem with goals is that the end result I want is often not attainable, especially within a fixed timeframe.

I'm not the only one that feels this way. My friend Matt Stone wrote a book titled *Goals Suck.* He argues that setting goals limits your potential because instead of doing your best, you are stressed out of your mind trying to meet deadlines and ambitious end results.

Matt says that a much better way of achieving is just discovering and doing what you love. Well, he was able to build six-figure business within a year with this attitude.

Another anti-goal man is Leo Babauta. He is a legend in the blogging world. He has more than a million followers of his *ZenHabits* blog. He also thinks goals limit your potential, believing that if you focus on a specific end result, you might miss the opportunity to create something bigger, better, or faster. The nature of goals limits their effects (see the etymology of the word). You can't aim in basketball to throw a 3-point shot and suddenly get 30 points. Leo argues that trying to achieve without goals frees you to accomplish more and can lead you to bigger and better end results via an unplanned route.

Matt's and Leo's accomplishments speak for themselves. And my humble results were achieved without goals too, which only confirms in my mind that there is some merit to a goal-less point of view. As I said about my personal mission statement and writing, I had no clue how to become a writer, but I did it. I hadn't have any writing goals. I didn't decide to publish a dozen books—or even two— in one year, or to sell two hundred or two million copies of my works.

But I achieved a specific number of books published and copies sold within a year, and I changed from wannabe to writer in my mind.

What is more, a lot of things happened that I hadn't anticipated up front. I earned a nice extra income, enough that I could get a mortgage for a house. I started tracking my habits in the Coach.me application and wrote a few habit plans for it. As a result, I became a coach and received support in writing my book from the members of the Coach.me community.

My conclusion: making goals is not a necessary step in achieving what you want. Sometimes they are downright hindering.

Goal-setting Approach

However, this coin also has another side. While the goals I've set have eluded me almost all my life, Jim Rohn, whom I respect immensely, was a big enthusiast of goals.

I tried to learn from him. I did the exercises he advised. My goal-achieving ratio didn't visibly improve. One thing is for sure, I'm not smarter than Jim Rohn. If he said it's good to have and pursue goals, I'm not quite ready to get rid of them altogether.

That's why I still bother with setting goals, writing them down, and following them. I set goals for 2014 and 2015 and failed miserably to reach them. I'm likely to repeat this experience in 2016. It won't stop me setting more goals in 2017.

Jim wasn't the only successful man who was fond of setting goals. Virtually all wildly successful people are. One of the most renowned goal-setting advocates is Brian Tracy. Others include John Maxwell, Zig Ziglar, and Anthony Robbins. This list goes on and on. Leo Babauta is an exception, not the rule. Clearly, no matter what I think about goal setting, the process works for some people. Anthony Robbins and Brian Tracy are not lunatics. If they are pro goal setting there is some merit in this concept. And this book series is about mimicking success, so I teach not only what works for me, but also what worked (and is working) for others on a large scale.

There is an urban myth doing the rounds about research showing that Harvard college students who had written goals were more successful after ten or twenty years than their peers without goals. This particular research has never been done. It's just a story that has been repeated so many times, it has become "known truth." However, common sense suggests that if such research *had* been performed, it would have had those results. Who is more likely to reach the destination, someone with a map or someone without it? Someone who knows where he is going or someone who has no clue?

Jim Rohn had an interesting story about financial goals. At the beginning of their relationship, his mentor, Earl Shoaff, asked Jim about his list of goals. He had none. Earl said: *"Then I can guess your bank account balance quite accurately."* And he did. This made Mr. Rohn do some thinking.

I have a similar story. The biggest amount of money I have ever saved without having goals was about €7,000. And it took me my whole adult life to amass such a sum. But in September 2012, I wrote down some goals for the first time since I was 18.

Only a few were financial and the targets were timid because I had no belief I could improve in that area. However, by July 2014 we had about €14,500 in our savings account. In less than a couple of years, I had more than doubled our savings.

We celebrated by spending almost all of it on purchasing our home, keeping only €1,000 for rainy days. A month later, I signed a contract with a publisher for the refurbishment of my old books, and the rainy day reserve was gone too.

By December 2014, I was scratching my head, wondering how to pay for the coal for winter. But I kept my habits in place, kept following my routines, and five months later, we were able to invest money into renovating our home, pay off the debt we took on in the previous year for the furniture, and have a big party for our daughter's First Communion.

We also were able to buy plane tickets to visit my parents in Ireland, and I bought my wife a separate car. (Yes, it was old, small, and dirt cheap, but still an investment we hadn't previously been able to afford.) And… we saved over €5,000. Needless to say, I now have my financial goals firmly written down. Earl Shoaff was on to something.

I do remember a few other times when I reached my goals. One such instance was when I published my first book. I gave myself five weeks for writing it and exactly on the set date, I finished the manuscript. I made some other goals after that to see the manuscript through to publishing, and I reached them all one by one.

Another of my goals was writing a compilation about Catholic Church teaching. I didn't set a deadline to complete this, but a nagging feeling developed, telling me I needed to finish so I could stop thinking about it. I wrote it between my fourth and fifth Kindle books. I shared it with just a few people. It's on my hard drive and a printed version is on my shelf. I got no tangible rewards from achieving this goal. On the other hand, I got the satisfaction of reaching it. It was one of those I set when doing goal exercises prescribed by Jim Rohn.

I've also failed many, many goals, multiple times. Each time I failed, I got a dose of frustration, but through the process of trying, I was closer to my goals than when I had set them.

In December 2013, I sold just 145 copies of my books. I wasn't impressed. Wanting to sell a *lot* more, I set a goal of selling 130,000 copies in 2014. Well, I managed to sell only 7,600, but it was four times more than I thought was **really** possible. I set what felt like an impossible goal, didn't accomplish it, but still generated a very good result.

Even when I don't achieve my goals, they surely protect me from complacency. As you can see, even a goal-resisting individual can extract some benefits from goal setting.

Today, I still set goals, but as doing so introduces frustration into my life, I limit their usage. I prefer to design a small daily discipline in accordance with the big goal and focus on those disciplines every day. That way I'm stressed and frustrated only on a tiny, daily scale.

This approach (tracking small, daily disciplines) moved me forward so far that I wouldn't have believed it if I hadn't experienced it. As I've already discussed, one of the more tangible goals I set for myself was to become a writer. Another goal connected to this one was that I wanted to be able to support my family just from my writing. I set goals in both 2014 and 2015 to quit my job during those years.

I didn't quit my job in 2014. It's now mid-2016 as I write this and nothing yet indicates a likelihood I'll be able to quit this year either. But while the income from my royalties is still lower than my salary, I'm earning real money. In 2014, I earned 11% of my salary. In 2015, I earned 48% of my salary. After 7 months of 2016, it's 24%. All this income has resulted from my discipline of writing every day.

I haven't missed my 400 word daily quota since the 26th of September 2013. Nowadays, I rarely write less than 1000 words a day. I'm a bit disappointed with my progress because I can't say farewell to my boss yet, but I don't fuss about it.

I fuss about writing every day. This is my focus. It moves me forward.

Which Method Will Serve You?

It's your job to figure out which approach works better for you. Maybe you should focus on specific goals or maybe it will be better for you to develop and implement a daily discipline. I can't impose the right solution on you. Only you can decide what will be more effective in your situation. With goals or without them, it's your responsibility to progress.

If you don't have any relevant experience to support a decision, choose one option (goal or discipline), pursue it, and pay attention to the results. Are you getting closer to what you want? Are you happy and satisfied in the process? Can you stick with this way indefinitely?

Sustainability is the ultimate indicator. If you can't keep your daily discipline or you can't live with the frustration caused by daunting goals, you won't persevere long enough to reap the fruits of whichever approach you are following.

Instead of Exercises

If you feel compelled to set your goals like a pro, I enumerated a few appropriate books in Recommended Books section. However, if you feel you absolutely must know my approach to goal setting visit ExpandBeyondYourself.com/goalsetting to obtain a chapter I extracted from this book, thinking that many authorities wrote so many volumes about this topic, that nobody will be interested in my ruminations. Well, prove me wrong. Once again, it's:

ExpandBeyondYourself.com/goalsetting

(Chapter SEVENTEEN)

Using Your Imagination

How can the images in your head transform your life?

I hope you've already grasped it: you are the source of your circumstances and your mind is the source of your actions (and more often, inactions!). Thus, if you can control what's going in your head, you are more likely to control what's happening in your life.

Can you use visualization wrongly? Of course you can. You have the power to use everything in your life in the service of good or evil. Your words, your body, and your thoughts can all be used to create harm. Visualization is not an exception.

Most of us use visualization wrongly by replaying in our heads past "movies"; we relive our lives again and again. Or we worry about the future, playing in our imagination catastrophic scenes that will never materialize.

When I was a shrinking violet, I tended to talk myself out of approaching any stranger. Usually my self-talk was accompanied by negative images, such as of women running around screaming, *"Pervert!"*

Like almost everything in your life, "good" and "bad" comes down to how well you exert conscious control over your behavior.

I don't like visualization, meditation, and all that intangible stuff. I love action. I tend to underutilize my imagination. Deep down, I despise it and I need to force myself to sit down and breathe or close my eyes and play a mind movie.

93

But we all know the "someday people," who spend too much time in their heads dreaming about a wonderful future that will never come because they don't do anything to materialize it.

You know yourself best and will know in which of above categories you belong. Act accordingly. If you rarely or never purposefully dream about things, you need, like me, to force yourself to sit your butt down, close your eyes, and train your brain's "muscles." If you are a daydreamer, you need to limit the time you spend inside your head or transform it into experiences that are more purposeful.

Why is Visualization So Darn Effective?
It's because we think in images. It's impossible to think a thought and not see it visually in your head. Every concept and experience is somehow translated into images. I read about an autistic guy who had an amazing talent with numbers. For example, he knew the number pi. He didn't just remember it, he knew it, like you know your image in the mirror. He said he saw different numbers as colors and their combinations.

An image is the first thing that appears in your mind whenever you think. It's a basic element of your thought process. If you can affect the images, you can affect the process and your whole life.

We undoubtedly have different capabilities when it comes to operating our imagination. When my sons were three and four, I observed a funny event illustrating this truism. Our younger son has always had a vivid imagination. He was playing next to his bed, talking about something, obviously engaged. His elder brother asked him:

"What are you doing?"

"I'm playing with a kitty," answered the younger. He had imagined a kitty and was apparently playing with the nonexistent

creature. That was so sweet! But his elder brother didn't understand the concept. Christopher is a down-to-earth fellow. An imaginary pet couldn't be seen, so it didn't exist. He got down on the floor and peeked under the bed:

"But, WHERE is the kitty?"

We have a lot of fun about this in our family, even a decade later.

The experiences we have when using our imagination will differ. For some it is fun and will bring almost instant results. For others (like me) it's a lot of effort and the effects are elusive. It takes a lot of energy to make images in my mind moving, clear, and colorful.

However, although it may be challenging, please practice using your imagination. Otherwise, it will use you, providing images that will accompany your negative self-talk.

The simplest and most effective technique, which I learned from an NLP trainer, is this: close your eyes and relax. Nothing more is necessary. You don't need a fancy recording or expansive video programs to teach you how to use your imagination.

Find two minutes, close your eyes, relax your body, breathe deeply, and play the movie in your head. I did that during my commute. Heck, I did that while running to the bus stop! My body was not relaxed, my eyes were open, but I flashed some images through my head while running.

Assuming you are less crazy than me, just close your eyes and relax.

Try to make the picture distinctly sharp. Try to employ other senses in your visualization: construct dialog in your head, smell the extravagant food you would like to taste, imagine the gentle wind from the ocean when you imagine your house on Hawaii.

Most important, add strong emotions to the mix. Feel a desire to reach your goals; feel the pleasure of getting what you want.

Whatever you imagine, remember that your mind hates cognitive dissonance. If you visualize one thing and do another, your brain will rebel. You will either abandon those impotent practices, go crazy, or start aligning your deeds to the words and images in your head. Again, I strongly recommend that you deliberately choose the path of aligning your words and deeds and keeping your mental competency!

There are other tools that utilize the graphical nature of our brains. You can create a vision board or a vision movie and watch them many times a day. I like their passive nature. I don't need to work mentally to absorb their message. I just watch. A vision board is especially handy in that regard. You can put it in a place that you scan often (like on the wall of your office or on the door of your closet) and automatically be affected by it (whenever you work or change your clothes).

A vision movie is just a vision board on steroids. You simply add some sound to the pictures. It can be done very simply. Just create a PowerPoint presentation and add some background music that stirs your emotions.

Whatever you decide to use to invigorate your imagination, do it regularly. I recommend practicing visualization at least once a day. I watch my vision board every morning. I also imagine speaking to engaged crowds for a few minutes a day, and I meet with Jim Rohn in my imagination, also once a day (and if you think that's weird, you should read *Think and Grow Rich!*).

Chapter EIGHTEEN

Using Your Skills and Strengths

Action and motivation are a bit like the chicken-egg riddle. Which was the first? Which was the cause and which was the result?

There are some who claim that action is a simple consequence of motivation. That first and foremost you should cultivate a high level of motivation and only then worry about action. With high enough motivation, action is frictionless. Zig Ziglar was a famous proponent of this approach:

"People often say that motivation doesn't last. Well, neither does bathing—that's why we recommend it daily."

In his book *Ziglar on Selling,* he instanced an experiment done by a drug expert, Forest Tennant, M.D., Dr.PH. The doctor took blood samples from five volunteers before and after one of Ziglar's speeches. The blood samples showed increased levels of endorphins and cortisol—simply from listening to a motivational speech.

There are some who claim that motivation is a myth, that it simply doesn't work. Those advancing this theory claim that only continued action can provide results and that neither "pep talks" nor "feeling motivated" have any effect. Stephen Guise, author of *Mini Habits,* is an advocate of this action-oriented worldview.

For me they are two edges of the same sword.

I can't imagine doing something without some kind of motivation. When we do something unpleasant, like going to school or to work, often it is due to negative motivation: *"I don't want my*

97

parents to scream at me," "I don't want to starve, I have to get money in this stinky job."

Negative or not, these factors are still motivating. I can't imagine being motivated and not taking action. Motivation and action are inseparable. I consider action more important only because it's so rare to find someone who is doing his job day in and day out, regularly and consistently.

It's more common to find someone who is "motivated," who has a mouth full of slogans, but isn't acting to support the slogans they spout. Think about your vision daily; take action towards it daily. At any one time, you may need to concentrate more on one than the other, but don't neglect either.

Design everyday habits that will keep your vision in front of your eyes AND actively bring you closer to the end result.

Purpose Makes a Difference

When I studied at university, I worked in a factory as a manual worker during my last summer vacation. Adam was a guy on our team. He did exactly the same job as everybody else in our production line, but you could sense he was different.

Adam did everything with extraordinary care and precision. He did the same things we all did, but he did them SO much better. What is more, he was not only focused on the work, but was gentle and humble. He had every bragging right—everybody knew he was the best among us—but he didn't brag at all. In fact, he was the quiet guy, always respectful, always attentive.

I got a chance to ask a colleague who had worked in the factory for a year or two about Adam. He told me Adam was the sole breadwinner for his family. His mother was very sick and he was doing all he could to support her. This was his motivation.

Here's another story I've heard from Jim Rohn in his *Cultivating an Unshakable Character* audio program. Victor Herman lived for about fifteen years in Russian work camps (those were designed to function like the death camps). The circumstances there were horrible. He survived only because he ate rat meat, mostly raw. Jim Rohn said that the thing that amazed him most about Victor's story was that he found the motivation to keep going entirely in himself.

Both Adam and Victor definitely had motivation, much deeper than ordinary men. They did extraordinary things because they were deeply motivated. Their purpose was pervasive, was a part of their essence to such an extent that they didn't even realize they had it.

Thus, if you are a living saint or the toughest man on Earth, you can safely skip any disciplines designed to cultivate motivation. If not, you would do well to begin some motivating habits right away.

Chapter NINETEEN

Your Direction Is Determined by Your Vision

The direction of your life is not determined in the most part by any skills or experience you've amassed. You can always learn new skills and gather new experience while doing it. I learned more about doing online business in the past three years than I learned about the economy in five years of university study. I learned how to create and manage a WordPress site, how to migrate between hosting providers, how to purchase a domain name, how to optimize posts for SEO, how to market and sell... Three years ago, I had no idea about any of it.

Of course, it's easier to leverage an area you are already familiar with. Instead of writing books, I really could crush it developing my IT career. All in all, I've already had eight years of experience.

But frankly, I'm sick of that. My vision is bigger than that.

I don't want to dwell on the mundane when there is more ahead. And I don't feel comfortable teaching others about something I don't have much success with. I know all too many authors who couldn't figure out how to make their books take off but then moved into teaching others how to write, publish, and market. I don't teach something I haven't done myself.

I encourage you to take inventory of your strengths, not of your skills. You were put into this world with a mission in mind and you are adequately equipped to fulfill that mission. Don't waste your powers, your time, or your talents chasing the things that don't fulfill. You are mortal. In the end, all the things you will gather won't serve you any longer.

Exercises

Think about what daily discipline you can introduce to train your focus. Brainstorm—take a pen and paper and write as many options as possible.

Then analyze your options. Discard anything you don't think you could persevere with for longer than 100 days. Pick at least one discipline today.

Repeat the exercise, this time brainstorming how you can discover your purpose, mission, or strengths. Again, pick one discipline that will be the easiest to sustain for a long period of time.

Do both disciplines (for example meditation and visualization) as soon as possible. If you can, do them right after figuring out your best choices. Plan how you will incorporate those disciplines into your daily life. Will you wake up five minutes earlier to perform them? Or maybe you will do them during the commute to work.

Write down your disciplines and your "performance plan." Track every day that you've stuck with your plan.

Chapter TWENTY

Using the Power of One

Are you a human? Well, the answer is quite obvious, isn't it? Of course you are!

But beyond that, the essence of you is not immediately obvious. What's the difference between a person who is illiterate and a person who simply doesn't read at all? Maybe in the definition there is a significant difference, but as neither read, there is no noticeable difference in their outputs.

What differentiates you from animals if you don't follow your purpose in life? Beasts also care about food and shelter and their cubs. But they rarely care about anything else. Don't bring yourself down to the animal level.

Live fuller. Look for your mission in life. Focus on it. We live in a wealthy society. Food and shelter are easy to get. Love and kindness aren't. Significance isn't.

If you live only to get by, to get food, shelter, and some entertainment, or even first-class meals, luxury shelter, and audacious entertainment, you will most probably end up being miserable. You are not an animal. You are created for greater things. Pursue them.

Engrave this equation into your soul:

TIME * ATTENTION = RESULTS

Success doesn't come from luck.

Multiply your time by developing and maintaining purposeful focus. The results you want will inevitably come. This is why focusing on one thing is so attractive. If you care about just one venture and invest your time into it, the results will materialize quickly.

If you divide your time and attention among many projects, results will still appear down the road, but you must have the patience to wait for them. When I started my business, I took eleven months to earn my first $1,000. I had no clue and my mindset was a shambles. It was a miracle that I achieved this success. Yet, I wasn't satisfied. I wanted more and faster results. I was ready to try every trick to get me on a faster route to success.

However, I couldn't force myself to concentrate 100% on just the publishing. My life is more than that. I appreciate all its facets. I have family, a wife, and kids who see me just a few hours each day, because I spend twelve hours working and commuting.

I don't want to neglect my spiritual life either: *"What, then, will anyone gain by winning the whole world and forfeiting his life?"*— **Mt 16: 26a**

I don't want to neglect relationships with my friends. If there is one main theme in my life, it's love and I'm trying to weave it into everything I do, including my books.

What's your "one thing?" Find it; target it; cling to it as if your life depends on it. Because it does. I don't mean so much your physical existence, but the quality of your life. Trust me, I led a purposeless life for many years; I know how it tastes.

A life without vision is incomparably worse than one with vision and purpose *"even if this cannot be achieved immediately and if what we are able to achieve, [...] is always less than we might wish"* —**Caritas in veritate, 78**

Train yourself in focus. You could start by meditating just a couple minutes a day. Or you could create a vision board illustrating what you want from life and who you want to become. Or you could visualize your great future for a few minutes a day. You could do all these things.

Just do something. Don't be insane. Insanity is doing the same over and over and expecting different results. You can't act the way average people do and become successful.

If you want to be a success, study success and listen to success. A staggering number of successful people recommend and practice meditation, visualizations, and vision boards.

If you want to be a successful writer, do what successful writers do: write. I started writing a moderate amount, regularly, and I achieved a moderate success. If you want to excel, exercise your key strength or practice your principal skills every single day. The more, the better. Remember the time factor in the success equation.

Activities like visualization and staring at vision boards probably won't bring you instant results. They may seem to be too "out there" to provide any results at all. But results will come. Rob Cubbon attributes his entire success to meditation practice. Pat Flynn was already a successful entrepreneur when he finally learned to meditate every day. His income jumped from five to six figures in less than half a year.

Don't pay too much attention to your initial results. Focus on your daily disciplines. Despite their elusive nature, they are perfectly trackable. Just keep yourself accountable: Did you meditate today? For how long? How many times did you look at your vision board? Did you imagine today that you were talking to crowds at a huge meeting?

Come up with just one discipline you can start today and track it for at least 100 days. Simultaneously, develop another discipline that will help you distill your purpose in life. Don't sit on your hands. Start right now and never stop.

You can do this. If I could transform myself from a man who was wandering without purpose into one who has meaning and direction, you can definitely do the same. And with the help of this book, you can do it faster and more effectively than I did.

Success is in you. And you are your success.

Godspeed.

< < < < The End > > > >

Connect with Michal

Thanks for reading all the way to the end. If you made it this far, you must have liked it! I really appreciate having people all over the world take interest in the thoughts, ideas, research, and words that I share in my books. I appreciate it so much that I invite you to visit www.ExpandBeyondYourself.com, where you can register to receive all of my future releases absolutely free.

Read a manifesto on my blog and if it clicks with you, there is a sign-up form at the bottom of the page, so we can stay connected.

Once again, that's www. ExpandBeyondYourself.com

More Books by Michal Stawicki

You can find more books by Michal at:

http://www.ExpandBeyondYourself.com/about/my-books/

A Small Favor

I want to ask a favor of you. If you have found value in this book, please take a moment and share your opinion with the world. Just let me know what you learned and how it affected you in a positive way. Your reviews help me to positively change the lives of others. Thank you!

About the Author

I'm Michal Stawicki and I live in Poland, Europe. I've been married for over fifteen years and am the father of two boys and one girl. I work full time in the IT industry, and recently, I've become an author. My passions are transparency, integrity, and progress.

In August 2012, I read a book called *The Slight Edge* by Jeff Olson. It took me a whole month to start implementing ideas from this book. That led me to reading numerous other books on personal development, some effective, some not so much. I took a look at myself and decided this was one person who could surely use some development.

In November of 2012, I created my personal mission statement; I consider it the real starting point of my progress. Over several months' time, I applied numerous self-help concepts and started building inspiring results: I lost some weight, greatly increased my savings, built new skills, and got rid of bad habits while developing better ones.

I'm very pragmatic, a down-to-earth person. I favor utilitarian, bottom-line results over pure artistry. Despite the ridiculous language, however, I found there is value in the "hokey-pokey visualization" stuff and I now see it as my mission to share what I have learned.

My books are not abstract. I avoid going mystical as much as possible. I don't believe that pure theory is what we need in order to change our lives; the Internet age has proven this quite clearly. What you will find in my books are:

- Detailed techniques and methods describing how you can improve your skills and drive results in specific areas of your life

- Real life examples

- Personal stories

So, whether you are completely new to personal development or have been crazy about the Law of Attraction for years, if you are looking for concrete strategies, you will find them in my books. My writing shows that I am a relatable, ordinary guy and not some ivory tower guru.

Recommended books:

- *The Slight Edge* by Jeff Olson

- *The 7 Habits of Highly Effective People* by Stephen R. Covey

- *Man's Search for Meaning* by Victor E. Frankl

- *Psycho-Cybernetics* by Maxwell Maltz

- *Goals Suck* by M.F. Stone

- *Stop Goal Setting* by J D Yoder

- *Productivity Unleashed* by Mark Messick

- *S.M.A.R.T. Goals Made Simple* by S.J. Scott

- *Mini Habits* by Stephen Guise

  And a couple of **my books** complementary to *Directed by Purpose*:

- *The Art of Persistence*

- *Know Yourself Like Your Success Depends of It*

  You may also want to check the first (and free) volume of this series:

- *Simplify Your Pursuit of Success*

Made in the USA
Las Vegas, NV
09 March 2021

19311785R00066